Presented to

_____

By

_____

On

_____

The Holy Spirit will come to you, and your child shall be called the Son of God. He shall rule a kingdom that will last forever.

— Luke 1:35

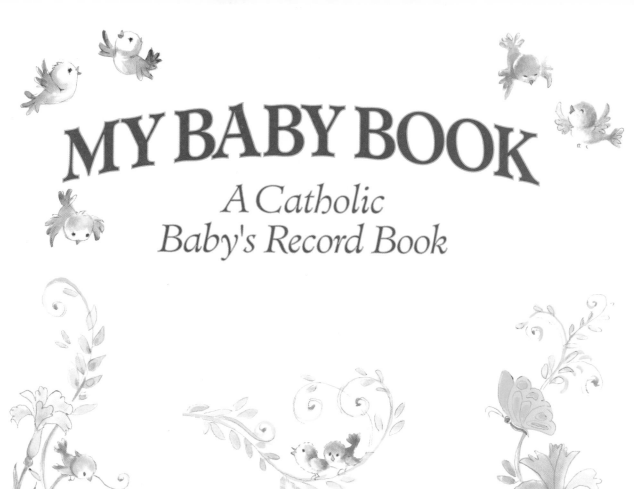

MY BABY BOOK

A Catholic
Baby's Record Book

Illustrated by
Rafaella Zanolin Blanc

The Regina Press
New York

Table of Contents

My Birth Certificate

And Jesus called to them, saying, "Let the children come to me, and do not hinder them, for to such belongs the kingdom of God."

— Luke 18:16

My Birth

My name is _____

I was born at _____ o'clock _____ M

on _____ Date

at _____ Place

in _____ City, State

Doctor _____

Pediatrician _____

Nurses _____

I weighed _____ lbs. _____ ozs.

and measured _____ inches

My hair was _____ and my eyes were _____

I was named _____

because _____

_____

I was the _____ child

of (Father) _____

and of (Mother) _____

_____

My home was at _____

_____

_____

My First Photograph

"And a little child shall lead them."
— Isaiah 11:16

Visitors and Gifts

Name   Gift

_____   _____

_____   _____

_____   _____

_____   _____

_____   _____

_____   _____

_____   _____

_____   _____

_____   _____

_____   _____

_____   _____

_____   _____

_____   _____

_____   _____

_____   _____

_____   _____

_____   _____

_____   _____

_____   _____

_____   _____

_____   _____

_____   _____

_____   _____

_____   _____

_____   _____

My Family Tree

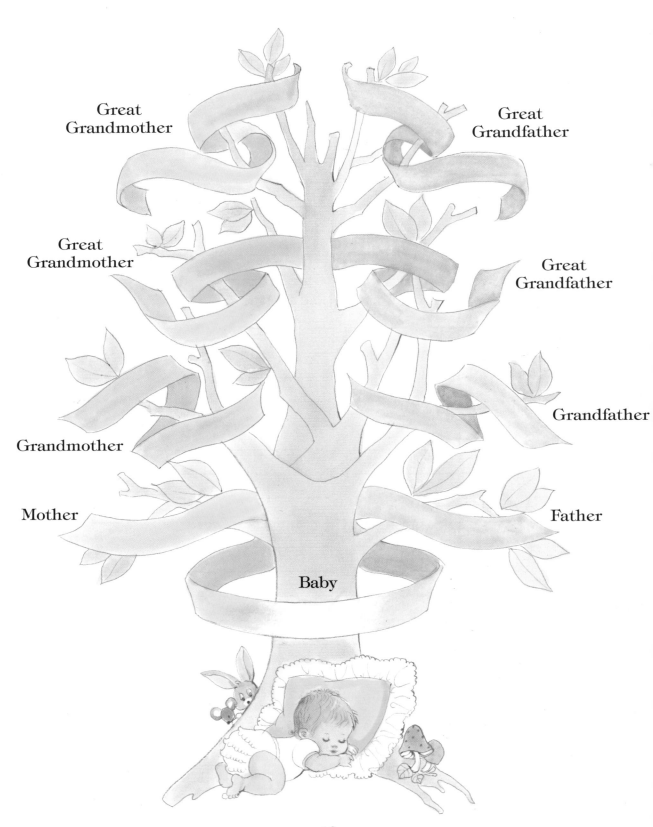

Great
Grandmother

Great
Grandfather

Great
Grandmother

Great
Grandfather

Grandmother

Grandfather

Mother

Father

Baby

My Relatives

Name   Relationship

_____   _____
_____   _____
_____   _____
_____   _____
_____   _____
_____   _____
_____   _____
_____   _____
_____   _____
_____   _____
_____   _____
_____   _____
_____   _____
_____   _____
_____   _____
_____   _____
_____   _____
_____   _____
_____   _____
_____   _____
_____   _____
_____   _____
_____   _____
_____   _____
_____   _____
_____   _____
_____   _____
_____   _____
_____   _____

I have baptized you in water; He will baptize you
in the Holy Spirit.

— Mark 1:8

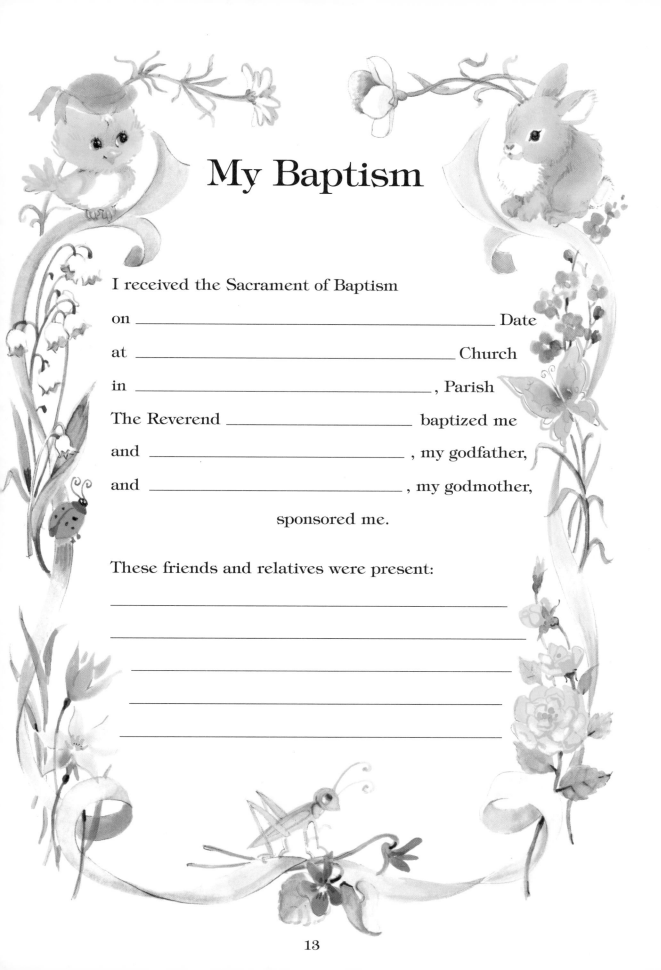

My Baptism

I received the Sacrament of Baptism

on _____ Date

at _____ Church

in _____ , Parish

The Reverend _____ baptized me

and _____ , my godfather,

and _____ , my godmother,

sponsored me.

These friends and relatives were present:

_____

_____

_____

_____

_____

"O sing to the Lord a new song, for he has done marvelous things."

— Psalm 98:1

14

My Early Development

MEMORABLE FIRSTS   Date

Held my head up _____

Turned my head _____

Had a bath _____

Recognized my mother _____

Recognized my father _____

Rolled over _____

Ate solid food _____

Recognized objects _____

Sat up _____

Crawled on all fours _____

Pulled myself up _____

Steps taken _____

Sounds uttered _____

Words spoken _____

Haircut _____

Tooth _____

Drew a picture _____

Began to count _____

Playmates _____

OTHER FIRSTS _____

_____

_____

_____

_____

_____

_____

_____

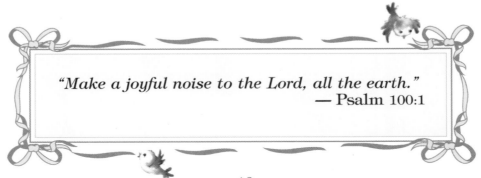

"Make a joyful noise to the Lord, all the earth."
— Psalm 100:1

My Favorite Things

Toys _____

_____

_____

Clothes _____

_____

Pets _____

_____

Games _____

_____

Stories _____

_____

Prayers _____

_____

_____

Songs _____

_____

_____

T.V. Show _____

_____

_____

Playmates _____

_____

_____

Other Favorites _____

_____

_____

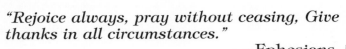

"Rejoice always, pray without ceasing, Give thanks in all circumstances."

— Ephesians 5:16

Other Memorable Firsts

My Mother and Father taught me how to pray
as a child. This is the first prayer I ever learned.

_____

_____

In time, I learned these important prayers.

_____ Age _____

_____ Age _____

_____ Age _____

On _____ at the age of _____

my Mother and Father brought me to _____

_____ Church

in _____

On _____ at the age of _____

I began my religious education at _____

_____ School

in _____

I was in _____ grade and my teacher was

_____

I attended my first Mass on _____

at _____ Church

in _____

The Reverend _____ was the celebrant.

I was _____ years old and these members of the family

were present: _____

_____

_____

_____

Other Sacraments I Have Received

Reconciliation

I received the Sacrament of Reconciliation at the age of _____

on _____

at _____ Church

in _____ .

The Reverend _____ heard my confession

Confirmation

I became a soldier of Christ on _____

at _____ Church

in _____ .

I was _____ years old.

Bishop _____ confirmed me.

and _____ was my sponsor.

I took the name of _____ in Confirmation.

These members of the family were present: _____

_____

_____

_____

_____

_____

_____

First Holy Communion

I received Jesus in the Eucharist for the first time _____

on _____

at _____ Church

in _____ Parish.

I was _____ years old.

The Reverend _____ celebrated the Mass, and

The Reverend _____ gave me communion.

These members of the family were present: _____

_____

_____

_____

_____

_____

_____

_____

_____

_____

This day in David's city a savior has been born to you, the Messiah and Lord.

— Luke 2:11

My First
Christmas

"For the love of Christ urges us on."
— II Corinthians 5:14

My Travels
and Vacations

"We are God's children now, what we will be has not been revealed."

— I John 3:2

My First Birthday

Second Birthday

_____
_____
_____
_____
_____
_____
_____
_____

Third Birthday

_____
_____
_____
_____
_____
_____
_____

Fourth Birthday

_____
_____
_____
_____
_____
_____

Fifth Birthday

_____
_____
_____
_____
_____
_____
_____
_____

Sixth Birthday

_____
_____
_____
_____
_____
_____
_____
_____
_____
_____
_____
_____

Seventh Birthday

_____
_____
_____
_____
_____
_____
_____

He grew in wisdom and age and grace before God and men.

— Luke 2:52

My Growth Chart

	Pounds and Ounces	Feet and Inches
Birth	_____	_____
1 Month	_____	_____
2 Months	_____	_____
3 Months	_____	_____
4 Months	_____	_____
5 Months	_____	_____
6 Months	_____	_____
7 Months	_____	_____
8 Months	_____	_____
9 Months	_____	_____
10 Months	_____	_____
11 Months	_____	_____
1 Year	_____	_____
1½ Years	_____	_____
2 Years	_____	_____
2½ Years	_____	_____
3 Years	_____	_____
3½ Years	_____	_____
4 Years	_____	_____
5 Years	_____	_____
6 Years	_____	_____
7 Years	_____	_____

"Bless the Lord, O my soul."

— Psalm 103:22

My Dental Chart

Central Incisor, 7½ months

Lateral Incisor, 9 months

Cuspid, 18 months

First Molar, 14 months

Second Molar, 24 months

First Permanent Molar, 6 years

First Permanent Molar, 6 years

Second Molar, 20 months

First Molar, 12 months

Cuspid 16 months

Lateral Incisor, 7 months

Central Incisor, 6 months

Visits to the Dentist

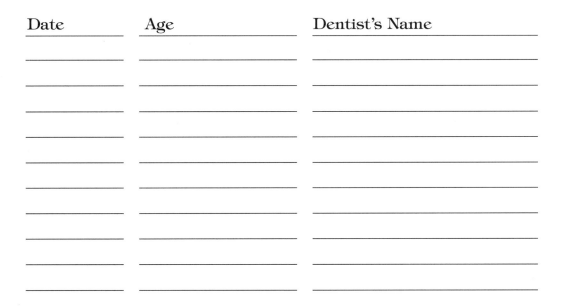

Date	Age	Dentist's Name

My Illnesses

Age	Type	Doctor's Name

My Medical Record

Immunizations	Date of Boosters	Series Completed	Doctor's Name
Diphtheria	_____	_____	_____
Tetanus	_____	_____	_____
Whooping Cough	_____	_____	_____
Measles	_____	_____	_____
Mumps	_____	_____	_____
Rubella	_____	_____	_____
Polio	_____	_____	_____
Other	_____	_____	_____
_____	_____	_____	_____
_____	_____	_____	_____

dpt { Diphtheria, Tetanus, Whooping Cough

mr { Measles, Mumps, Rubella

Tests	Date	Doctor's Name
Tuberculin	_____	_____
Other	_____	_____
_____	_____	_____
_____	_____	_____

Blood Type _____

Allergies	Doctor's Name	Remarks
_____	_____	_____
_____	_____	_____
_____	_____	_____
_____	_____	_____
_____	_____	_____

"*For I am the Lord who heals you.*"
— **Exodus 15:26**

My Visits
to the Doctor

Date	Age	Remarks

"*Happy are those who find wisdom, and those who get understanding...She is a tree of life to those.*"

— Proverbs 3:13

My Schooling

Nursery School

_____
_____
_____
_____
_____
_____
_____
_____

Kindergarten

_____
_____
_____
_____
_____
_____
_____

First Grade

_____
_____
_____
_____
_____
_____
_____
_____

Second Grade

_____
_____
_____
_____
_____
_____
_____
_____
_____
_____

Third Grade

_____
_____
_____
_____
_____
_____
_____

Fourth Grade

Fifth Grade

Sixth Grade

Photos

"Give us each day our daily bread."
— Luke 11:13

Colophon